David

By Cristina Marques

SCANDINAVIA

INTRODUCTION

Jesus said, "Become like little children." The Children of the Bible series puts attention on the littlest of Jesus' flock. Each of these characters has an inspiring story to tell. God used their lives to teach the world about his love. As you read these stories aloud, remember God's presence inside every child's spirit. The simplest stories sometimes hold the greatest power. May these stories be the beginning of a lifelong love of the Bible for your children. There is treasure to gain for young and old alike.

DAVID

(1 SAMUEL 16-17)

David was the youngest of his family. He grew up loving God. He also loved being a shepherd. He was always taking care of his father's flock.

A prophet named Samuel came to their town.

God told Samuel, "Go to the home of a man named Jesse. I have chosen one of his sons to be the new king of Israel."

One by one, Jesse presented his sons while David was in the field. God did not approve of any of them.

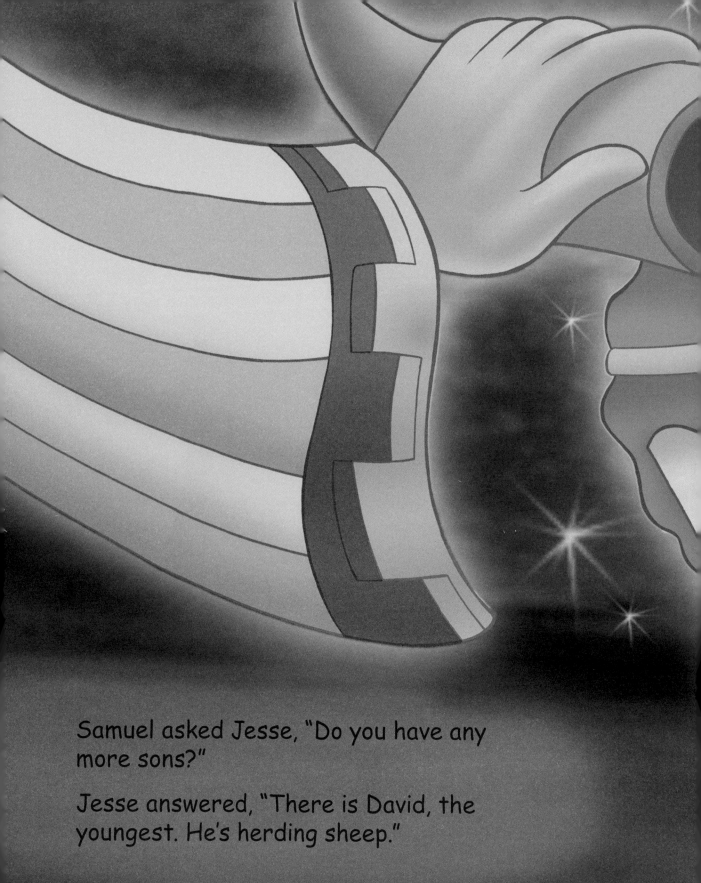

Samuel asked Jesse, "Do you have any more sons?"

Jesse answered, "There is David, the youngest. He's herding sheep."

Samuel sent for David.

As David came running up, God spoke to Samuel. He said, "Anoint him. He is the one I have chosen."

God was with David as he grew up.

One day the Philistines attacked Israel. David's brothers left for battle. Their father sent David to check on them.

David found his brothers in the army camp. An enemy named Goliath was teasing them from across the field. Goliath was a giant! The soldiers were afraid.

But David got angry. "He is laughing at God's own army," he said. "I'll fight him!"

David went to a nearby brook. He chose five smooth stones. He put them in his shepherd's bag. Then he ran back to Goliath.

"I'm ready to fight!" David shouted.

But Goliath just laughed. "Am I a dog? Are you going to throw stones at me?"

David answered, "You may have a sword and spear. But I come with the Lord God on my side."

David reached in his bag. He grabbed a stone and put it in his slingshot. He aimed and hit Goliath right in the forehead. Goliath fell over and hit the ground.

David was only a shepherd boy. But his love of God gave him the courage to fight. Now he had beaten Goliath, the giant. God was with him.

DAVID - COURAGE

David was only a boy. Yet David showed that size is not what counts. His brothers were afraid. David was afraid, too. But he had the courage to fight Goliath because he trusted in the Lord.
God honored this courage.
The Lord can do anything! David knew God takes care of those who believe. Take courage in God. You can do the impossible, too.

© Scandinavia Publishing House
Drejervej 15,3 DK - Copenhagen NV Denmark
Tel. (+45) 3531 0330
www.scanpublishing.dk
info@scanpublishing.dk
All rights reserved.

Text: Cristina Marques
Illustrations and graphic design:
Belli Studio, Gao Hanyu
Translation: Ruth Marschalek, Lissa Jensen

Printed in China
ISBN: 978 87 7247 173 0